Perfect for Youngsters and Adults

Master the Art of Machine Prompt Engineering

Unlock AI for Life, Business, and Career Success

Ijigban Daniel Oketa

Copyright

All rights reserved.© 2024 by Ijigban Daniel Oketa

Master the Art of Machine Prompt Engineering:
Unlock AI for Life, Business, and Career Success

No part of this book may be reproduced, distributed, or transmitted in any form or by any means, including photocopying, recording, or other electronic or mechanical methods, without the prior written permission of the author, except in the case of brief quotations embodied in critical reviews and certain other non-commercial uses permitted by copyright law.

For permissions requests, please contact the author at:
oketadaniels@gmail.com   www.idoketa.com

This book is a work of non-fiction. While the author has made every effort to ensure accuracy, the information provided is offered on an "as is" basis and without warranties of any kind. Readers are encouraged to use their discretion and seek professional advice where necessary.

Published by:
TFDC Publishers

ISBN: 9798304412407
First Edition: November 2024

Cover Design: Self-Designed
Image: AI ChatGT Generated

Printed in Nigeria/Amazon Bookstore .
All inquiries should be directed to:
oketadaniels@gmail.com +234703-738-4814

Table of Contents

Chapter One: Introduction – Unlocking the Future with AI and Online Wealth.....4

Chapter Two: How to Start Making Money Online: Your Step-by-Step Guide. 8

Chapter Three: Mastering Machine Prompt Engineering – Your AI Superpower.............................13

Chapter Four: The Creator Consciousness – Transform Challenges into Opportunities................37

Chapter Five: The Good Life Philosophy – Crafting and Sharing Your Path to Success................... 47

Chapter Six: My Journey: The Birth of a Transformative Idea..............58

Chapter Seven: Mastering Machine Prompt Engineering: Key to Innovation, Iteration and Evolving.......... 68

Chapter Eight: Conclusion – Embrace the Power Within..................... 72

Chapter One: Introduction – Unlocking the Future with AI and Online Wealth

Are you ready to tap into the boundless opportunities of making money online? The digital revolution has transformed how money is made or created, and at its core lies a powerful tool: **Artificial Intelligence (AI).**

AI is no longer confined to the tech sector—it has become a universal enabler across industries. Whether you're a budding entrepreneur, an established business leader, a professional, or a student, AI can redefine your potential and pave the way to new opportunities. This is not about coding or having to write any code or design.

For example, this entire book was conceived and written and packaged within 24hours through the help of AI.. This is your guide to leveraging AI to elevate your thoughts, business, and career. It's about unlocking the power of AI to create wealth, transform your mindset, and design the life you've always dreamed of.

The Path to Online Success: making money in today's digital age isn't just about talent or hard work—it's about knowing how to use the tools at your disposal. Here's an outline of how this book will empower you to get started and scale fast:

1. **Start Creating Content.** Content is king in the online world, and creating valuable content can open the doors to multiple streams of income.

2. **Master Machine Prompt Engineering.** This isn't about coding—it's about crafting precise instructions to unlock the potential of AI to establish profitability in your business and career.

3. **Adopt the Creator Mentality** Success starts in the mind as a mindset. The core is to move away from a victim mentality or fixed mindset to embrace a **creator consciousness** for transformative breakthrough.

4. **Create Your Good Life Philosophy.** What works for you can work for others. By reflecting on your experiences and identifying principles that have led to success, you can craft a philosophy of life that's both personal and universal. This philosophy can be monetized or shared to inspire others, helping them achieve their dreams while adding value to your own journey.

5. **Turn Challenges to Opportunities. Never Give Up.** Life comes with its challenges, but persistence and flexibility are essential to reaching your goals. Learn from my journey—a story of resilience, innovation, and transformation.

Who This Book Is For? This understanding is designed for anyone looking to elevate their life, business, or career, including:

- **Entrepreneurs:** Scale your ventures with AI and online tools.
- **Business Leaders:** Optimize operations, innovate, and grow your brand.
- **Professionals:** Enhance your skills and stand out in your field.
- **Students:** Learn future-proof skills and start earning while you study.

Why AI is the Future: AI mastery, especially through Machine Prompt Engineering, is your fast track to online wealth. It allows you to transform your ideas into income, optimize every aspect of your business or career, and create new possibilities.

The best part is that the AI tools are accessible, and the opportunities are limitless. The future belongs to those who act in the present times.

Take control of your destiny by investing in skills that will define success in the years to come.

This is not just a transformative guide—it's a call to action. So the goal is to help you start transforming your life with AI. And leverage it to:

- Generate income online.
- Redefine your mindset for success.

- Inspire others while building your legacy.

The journey begins here. The power is in your hands.

Congratulations!!!

Your Success Friend,
Ijigban Daniel Oketa

Chapter Two: How to Start Making Money Online: Your Step-by-Step Guide

Let me use my case scenario here. Just as I mentioned earlier; this entire book was conceived and then made with the help of AI (particularly ChatGT) in less than 24hours through machine prompt engineering which I am going to show you right here.

By the time you are reading or going through this work; it should have made me hundreds, thousands or tens of thousands of dollars through its distribution online and offline. And it should have also given me an edge in many ways even as an AI Tools or Machine Prompt Engineering Consultant.

You see, it may be understatement to say the internet offers limitless opportunities to generate income, and this is the perfect time to leverage technology for financial success.

Whether you're a beginner or looking to scale, the key lies in creating valuable and engaging content consistently with the help of AI and then you may scale otherwise. The truth is that you need AI, especially machine prompt engineering in all you do.

Here's how you can get started:

1. Write and Publish Online Content

What to Do: Share your knowledge, experiences, or insights by writing articles, essays, or blog posts. Platforms like **Medium**, **Substack**, or your own blog are excellent for building a readership and monetizing your content through ads, subscriptions, or affiliate marketing.

Topics to Explore:

- How-to guides or tutorials.
- Personal stories that inspire or teach lessons.
- Opinion pieces on current events or industry trends.
- Niche topics like tech reviews, travel, or personal finance.

Why It Works: Writing builds authority and attracts a loyal audience. Over time, consistent content creation can turn your platform into a passive income stream.

2. Create Video Content

What to Do: Video is one of the most engaging content formats today. Start a YouTube channel, Facebook page, or TikTok account to share your ideas. Monetize through ads, sponsored content, or selling products/services.

Ideas for Video Content:

- Tutorials and how-tos (e.g., using AI tools, fitness routines, cooking)

- Inspirational content (e.g., personal growth stories, motivational talks)
- Entertainment (e.g., challenges, skits, or travel vlogs)
- Product reviews or unboxings

Why It Works: Videos connect more emotionally with audiences and have higher potential to go viral. Platforms like YouTube, Facebook also reward creators with ad revenue.

3. Blog About Trends

What to Do: Create a blog or website focused on trending topics. By staying ahead of what people are searching for, you can generate traffic and earn income through ad placements, sponsored posts, or affiliate links.

Trending Areas to Focus On:

- Technology and AI advancements
- Climate change and sustainability
- Pop culture, movies, and music
- News and political updates
- Health and wellness trends

Why It Works: When you create content around trends, you capitalize on high-interest topics that can attract large audiences quickly in any of the platforms you choose..

Action Plan: Consistency is Key

No matter which path you choose, regular content creation is crucial to building an audience and staying relevant. Aim to publish **daily** or at least **three times a week** to maintain momentum.

Pro Tip: Master the Art of Machine Prompt Engineering

Although, we shall explore deeply in the next chapter. Incorporating AI into your content creation process is the ultimate game-changer. With tools like ChatGPT, you can:

- Generate blog post ideas or outlines in seconds.
- Automate research for current trends.
- Draft scripts, captions, and descriptions effortlessly.
- Edit and refine content with high precision.

What is Machine Prompt Engineering?
It's the skill of crafting effective prompts to get the best results from AI tools. For example:

- Instead of asking or telling ChatGPT to, *"Write about blogging,"* you could say, *"Create a detailed blog outline on how beginners can earn through affiliate marketing with examples and statistics."*

Why Learn Machine Prompt Engineering? Mastering Machine Prompt Engineering ensures your content stands out, is relevant, and is created faster, giving you a competitive edge.

Extra Tips to Maximize Success:

- **Invest in tools:** Use platforms like Canva for designs or SEO tools like Ahrefs.
- **Build a network:** Collaborate with other creators to grow faster.
- **Engage with your audience:** Reply to comments and adapt content to what they love.

Start now, stay consistent, and leverage AI to revolutionize your online content journey. Success awaits!

Now let's jump into the nitty-gritty of machine prompt engineering and how to use it like I do or even better to achieve more.

Chapter Three: Mastering Machine Prompt Engineering – Your AI Superpower

Imagine having an understanding that could help you instantly brainstorm ideas, write persuasive copy, or generate innovative solutions. That's the power of Machine Prompt Engineering (MPE).

This skill doesn't require coding but focuses on crafting precise prompts to unlock AI's full potential.

Whether you're an entrepreneur, professional, or student, mastering MPE can revolutionize how you work, create, and grow.

What is Machine Prompt Engineering?

Machine Prompt Engineering is the art of asking AI the right questions to get specific, actionable, and high-quality responses.

It's like giving instructions to an expert assistant who can instantly analyze data, generate ideas, and solve problems.

Think of prompts as the "magic words" that direct AI to:

- Write an engaging blog post.
- Create a business plan.

- Develop a marketing strategy.
- Generate innovative product ideas.
- Analyze a concept.
- Suggest project titles or implementation strategies.

Machine prompt engineering technically means "the better your prompts, the better the output."

How I Use Machine Prompt Engineering

I have created or written books, agreements, articles, business plans, project and product ideas in minutes against days or weeks. Here are the ways and examples of how I use machine prompt engineering with ChatGPT (for example):

1. **Grants and Project Design:** I copy the special grant goal or thematic areas or important points into MS word (to edit) or directly into the ChatGPT with prompts such as:

    a. Suggest five projects to be executed in line with the thematic areas
    b. Put a social location and year-term (if need be).
    c. Combine number 1 and 5 Project into one (if there is need)
    d. Write or Create the Project (1, 5 2 etc) or the combined one.

2. **Business Plans:** just like the above, you need to do is to feed the AI tool with the requirements or feature of the business plan you want such as:

    a. Title,
    b. Subject
    c. Business entity
    d. Budget etc

3. **Articles or Storyline**: you can write a creative article by doing the doing the following:

    a. Create a short story or narrative and ask as ChatGPT to refine and develop.
    b. You can refine your prompt as much as possible to bring out the feathers.
    c. Copy to Ms word- add or sub it your own and then ask chat G

    For example, in the chapter of this book "My Journey", I wrote a story line as much as I could. I then copied it to Chatgpt to "refine and expand it" and you can see; it makes the story catchy, adding sections to it. It can still be refined and expanded with more prompts. That's the beauty and it can make up a book or be added to a book.

4. **Books:** AI can help you to write your book or books in the same manner: for example, you could:

a. Ask ChatGPT to "**give me 5 book trending titles about a marriage success**" or a theme or areas you want.

b. Select a title or refine the title yourself, ask it to "Develop Table of Content or it.

c. Copy each developed table of content and ask to write it out for you. You can still add a narrative or story line for it to "expand" or "refine" for you based on the chapter.

As you go on, you can refine the prompt as much as you want. AI does not work effectively without your mind and the best way is to leverage the power of machine prompt engineering.

Tip to Creating Images: For example, instead of telling an AI tool to "create two different pictures of me with different clothes and postures", you could refine and say:

"Create 2 different pictures of me (photo attached) with different clothes and postures.
Outfits: 1 Formal and 1 traditional.
Postures: 1 formal picture of me sitting on a table in an executive office working smiling, etc.
Postures: 1 traditional picture of me standing, arms crossed, smiling."

Use the Attached picture to look more alike (then you attach an existing picture to look more like the original. In this case, the picture failed to bring out my resemblance but I could if I kept trying.

The second prompt engineering or descriptions will help AI to create the images for you. I was using the free version of ChatGPT (though limited to number of pictures and other creative arts for five hours); the prompt gave me the following images:

"AI does not work effectively without your mind and the best way is to leverage the power of machine prompt engineering."

All these should make you understand machine prompt engineering. However, let's elaborate more. And the following was written by ChatGPT itself and refined by me.

More Examples of How Machine Prompt Engineering Empowers You

1. **Copyrighting:**
   AI can generate compelling ad copies, taglines, and engaging social media posts, saving time and increasing creativity.

Pro Tips:

- **Start with clear instructions:** *"Write a catchy Facebook ad for a fitness app targeting millennials."*

- **Include tone details:** *"Make it witty and persuasive."*

- **Use AI to test variations:** *"Create five versions of this tagline emphasizing health benefits."*

Secret Tip: Combine AI output with personal tweaks to add authenticity and brand alignment.

2. **Grant and Proposal Writing:**
   AI can help you craft well-structured proposals and grants tailored to the requirements of funders.

Pro Tips:

- Include specific criteria: *"Draft a 500-word grant proposal for a community health project, focusing on measurable outcomes and sustainability."*

- Use prompts to refine: *"Reorganize this proposal to highlight the impact and feasibility more prominently."*

- Request formatting help: *"Format this as per USAID guidelines."*

Secret Tip: Ask AI for examples of successful proposals in your field for inspiration.

3. **Digital Marketing:**
   From generating campaign ideas to analyzing performance, AI becomes your ultimate marketing assistant.

Pro Tips:

- **Strategy development:** *"Outline a social media strategy for launching a new eco-friendly product."*
- **Content ideas:** *"Generate 10 Instagram post ideas for a skincare brand."*
- **Performance analysis:** *"Analyze these metrics and suggest optimizations for better engagement."*

Secret Tip: Use AI to personalize messages for different audience segments, increasing relevance and conversion rates.

   4. **Business and Product Development:**
      AI can simplify brainstorming, planning, and strategizing for new ventures or products.

Pro Tips:

- Brainstorming: *"List 20 innovative ideas for a tech startup focused on sustainability."*

- Market analysis: *"Summarize the trends in the electric vehicle industry and suggest market gaps."*

- Product descriptions: *"Write a product description for a smartwatch highlighting health tracking and connectivity."*

Secret Tip: Use prompts to simulate customer feedback: *"Pretend you are a user of this product. What features would you want improved?"*

Applications Across Various Fields

The following are more ways we can deploy machine prompt engineering to achieve your goals.

   1. **Education:** Use AI to create lesson plans, quizzes, or explain complex topics.

Prompt: *"Explain the concept of quantum physics in simple terms for a high school student."*

2. **Content Creation:** Generate ideas, outlines, and drafts for blogs, eBooks, or video scripts.
   Prompt: *"Outline a 10-chapter eBook on financial literacy for beginners."*

3. **Personal Development:** Plan goals, daily schedules, or personal growth strategies.
   Prompt: *"Create a 30-day self-improvement plan focusing on productivity and health."*

4. **Problem-Solving:** Address specific challenges in your business or personal projects.
   Prompt: *"Suggest ways to increase customer retention in an online store." "How do I recreate myself in others to do what I want"*

5. **Legal Profession:** to create agreement, quote relevant portions of the constitution or align.
   Prompt: *considering section 34 and 35 of the Nigerian Constitution to create my defense in Court of Law and or secondly a paper for public hearing in the National Assembly.*

6. **Medical Profession:** Use AI to assist with patient education, research, or drafting professional materials.
   Prompt: *"Explain the symptoms, causes, and treatment options for diabetes in simple terms for patient education."*

> **Prompt:** *"Draft a research outline on the impact of AI in diagnosing rare diseases."*

7. **Internet Tech –No Code:** There are many AI powered tools for creative websites and apps without writing any code. All you need is to choose your domain and services, pay and the rest is history.

There is no end in sight for how much and where we can use machine prompt engineering. The earlier you start mastering it; the better it is for you. Work smart. I was able to add to the above and you may not know the difference because I have mastered the art of effective prompts.

Mastering the Art of Effective Prompts

To make the most of Machine Prompt Engineering, follow these principles:

1. **Be Specific:** Clearly define what you want.
   Example: Instead of *"Write about marketing,"* say, *"Write a 500-word article on influencer marketing for small businesses."*

2. **Add Context:** Provide details to improve accuracy.
   Example: *"Suggest budget-friendly marketing strategies for a local bakery in a small town."*

3. **Iterate:** Refine and tweak prompts based on output.
   Example: *"Make the tone more conversational."*

4. **Use Examples:** Help AI understand by referencing samples.
   Example: *"Write a tweet like this: [Insert sample tweet]."* or *"Recreate this Article [insert sample]"*

When you think about a prompt; do not hold back- give it to the AI; she is always capable of giving you more suggestions or refining it for you.

Why Machine Prompt Engineering Matters

Just like the internet, today and beyond, AI will continue to be a critical tool for the way we will work or make money and to establish our success. By mastering Machine Prompt Engineering, you can:

- Save time by automating repetitive tasks.
- Enhance creativity with unique ideas and solutions.
- Stay competitive in a rapidly evolving digital landscape.
- Make more money or refine the way you make money online or offline.

Machine Prompt Engineering is not just a skill—it's a gateway to leveraging AI for endless possibilities. Whether you're creating, strategizing, or problem-solving, the right prompt can unlock the answers you need. Start practicing today and watch as AI becomes your most valuable partner in achieving success.

Using AI means you will work but more creatively and with better output and speed by mastering machine prompt engineering. You can take a complete newsline or story and rewrite it with more insight or lessons.

Re-Engineering Your Prompts

Artificial Intelligence is only as powerful as the instructions you give it. The quality of the output depends on how clear and specific your input is. This is where the art of crafting effective prompts comes in. Think of prompts as the bridge between your ideas and the AI's capabilities. The better your prompts, the better the results you'll get, whether you're creating content, solving problems, or exploring new ideas.

Let me show you why I mean right here. I typed and copied the following into GhatGPT like this:

Prompt: Refine this: *"There are many other AI tools you can use to deploy Machine prompt engineering. ChatGPT is just a tip of the iceberg. Machine Prompt Engineering is the main usable power of AI Tools and you should maximize it freely. Your success with AI tools most times depends on your prompt engineering (not a paid version) to get the best of an AI tool."*

Here is the answer I got:

"There are countless AI tools available, and ChatGPT is just the beginning. The real power of AI lies in Machine Prompt Engineering—the art of crafting precise and effective prompts to unlock the full potential of these tools. Success with AI tools often hinges not on paid versions but on your ability to master prompt engineering, enabling you to maximize their capabilities for free."

Then I followed up and prompted it again saying **"Use Simple words and language"**. Here is the result:

"There are many AI tools out there, and ChatGPT is just one of them. The real strength of AI comes from how well you can create clear and effective prompts—this is what Machine Prompt Engineering *is all about. Your success with AI tools doesn't depend on having a paid version but on how well you can ask the right questions to get the best results."*

From the above results, you may choose or expand the one you want. With your prompts, you can turn a statement or paragraph to a book or a course etc as you constantly refine or re-engineer it. With machine prompt engineering, you can also deploy your creator mentality and consciousness.

Re-engineering the Title of this Book

I am going to show how I re-engineered the title of this book through ChatGPT. This is to further illustrate how prompt engineering can help you in many areas through your creative insight and thoughts.

First of all, I tried to create the title of this book from the previous title since they are almost the same. So asked ChatGT to do the following:

"AI CONTENT CREATION MASTERY: *How to Advance Your Personal Life, Business and Career Through Creator Consciousness and Machine Prompt Engineering"*

Prompt: *Suggest five powerfully attractive titles that can replace the above for faster sales.*

ChatGPT replied:

1. **"Prompt to Profit:** *Master AI Content Creation for Life, Business, and Career Success"*
2. **"AI Creator Secrets:** *Unlock Your Potential with Machine Prompt Mastery"*
3. **"Content Creation Unleashed:** *Boost Your Life and Business with AI Power"*
4. **"The AI Creator's Edge:** *Transform Your Career with Prompt Engineering"*
5. **"Mastering AI for Success:** *How to Dominate Content, Business, and Personal Growth"*

From the above, I asked ChatGPT as a suggestion:

"What about this title? *"Machine Prompt Engineering: Master AI for Life, Business, and Career Success"*

ChatGPT said:

Your suggested title, **"Machine Prompt Engineering: Master AI for Life, Business, and Career Success,"** is strong, clear, and compelling. It emphasizes mastery, practicality, and broad application, which appeals to a wide audience.

Here are a few slight refinements to make it even more engaging:

1. **"Master Machine Prompt Engineering:** Unlock AI for Life, Business, and Career Success"
2. **"Machine Prompt Engineering Made Simple:** Dominate AI for Personal and Professional Growth"
3. **"AI Mastery Through Machine Prompt Engineering:** Achieve Life, Career, and Business Breakthroughs"
4. **"Machine Prompt Engineering:** Your Ultimate Guide to AI-Driven Success"
5. **"The AI Advantage:** Master Machine Prompt Engineering for Business and Career Growth"

These variations maintain the core idea while tweaking the tone or structure to further enhance appeal. Let me know if you'd like me to refine it further!

My next response was: *I go with number 1: "Master Machine Prompt Engineering: Unlock AI for Life, Business, and Career Success"*

ChatGPT said:

"Great choice! The title is engaging and conveys both expertise and practicality. Let me know how else I can support your project!"

You may think it is all over but the next morning, while working on the book, I thought of rejuvenating the title once more so I asked ChatGPT saying

"As a title, can "The Art of Machine Prompt Engineering: Unlock AI for Life, Business, and Career Success" fit in against "Master Machine Prompt Engineering: Unlock AI for Life, Business, and Career Success" ? If yes or no, give reasons.

ChatGPT said:

"Both titles are compelling, but they differ slightly in tone and focus. Here's a breakdown of how they compare:

1. "The Art of Machine Prompt Engineering: Unlock AI for Life, Business, and Career Success"

- **Tone:** This title emphasizes creativity and a sense of finesse. Using "The Art" suggests that prompt engineering is a skill that combines both technical expertise and creative mastery.

- **Fit:** It appeals to readers who value artistry, nuance, and the idea of mastering a craft. It positions prompt engineering as a blend of science and creativity, which might attract a more visionary or creative audience.

- **Pros:** Inspires curiosity and evokes the idea of a unique and innovative approach.

- **Cons:** May not immediately communicate authority or technical mastery, as "art" can sound less structured to some audiences.

2. "Master Machine Prompt Engineering: Unlock AI for Life, Business, and Career Success"

- **Tone:** This title conveys authority, expertise, and a focus on actionable mastery. Using "Master" suggests a structured, comprehensive guide to becoming highly skilled in prompt engineering.

- **Fit:** It appeals to readers looking for confidence, practicality, and mastery in AI-related skills.

- **Pros:** Conveys professionalism, expertise, and direct applicability, making it more appealing to readers with clear, goal-oriented intentions.

- **Cons:** May feel slightly formal or rigid to audiences seeking a more creative or exploratory tone.

Conclusion

Both titles can work, but **"Master Machine Prompt Engineering"** has a more authoritative and professional tone, which is better suited for readers who want actionable knowledge and confidence in the subject.

"The Art of Machine Prompt Engineering" is more suited to a creative or philosophical audience who values innovation and finesse.

If you're targeting a broader, practical audience looking to implement AI skills quickly, **"Master Machine Prompt Engineering"** would be the better choice. If you're framing your content as both practical and inspirational, **"The Art of Machine Prompt Engineering"** could work well."

You may think I should stop here, but no I did not. After reading the above reply, I asked ChatGPT again.

"How about this title: "Master the Art of Machine Prompt Engineering Unlock AI for Life, Business, and Career Success"

ChatGPT said:

The title **"Master the Art of Machine Prompt Engineering: Unlock AI for Life, Business, and**

Career Success" strikes an excellent balance between the other two options. Here's why it works:

Strengths of This Title

1. **Combines Authority and Creativity**:
    - The phrase "Master the Art" conveys both technical mastery and creative finesse, appealing to a broader audience.
    - It frames prompt engineering as a skill worth refining, which resonates with both practical learners and those who appreciate the artistry behind innovation.

2. **Balanced Tone**:
    - It maintains a sense of authority ("Master") while adding a creative flair ("the Art"), making it versatile and attractive.

3. **Engaging and Inspirational**:
    - It motivates readers by suggesting they can achieve mastery and harness a powerful tool for transformative results in life, business, and career.

4. **Broader Appeal**:
    - This title caters to professionals, entrepreneurs, and creatives alike,

ensuring a wider audience is drawn to the guide.

Conclusion

This title is likely your best option. It's dynamic, versatile, and compelling, making it ideal for readers seeking actionable insights, innovation, and inspiration. It's the perfect blend of the professional tone in **"Master Machine Prompt Engineering"** and the creative nuance in **"The Art of Machine Prompt Engineering."**

End…

From the above, this is how I arrived at a refined title of this book (a bit distinct from the others). And you can see it is better. This shows you how not to limit yourself but to keep refining or re-engineering your prompts. In life generally, it also shows you should keep refining your thoughts with actions until you reach your goal.

List of AI Tools

Here's a list of over 20 AI tools for content creation, along with their specific uses or focuses:

1. **ChatGPT (OpenAI)** - Generates conversational text, writes articles, answers questions, and assists with brainstorming. https://openai.com/chatgpt

2. **Jasper AI** - Specialized in copywriting, blogging, and creating SEO-focused marketing content. https://www.jasper.ai

3. **Writesonic** - Creates ad copies, blog posts, and product descriptions. https://writesonic.com

4. **Copy.ai** - Focuses on sales emails, social media posts, and taglines. https://www.copy.ai

5. **Canva Magic Write** - Writes captions, headlines, and short-form content directly within Canva designs. https://www.canva.com

6. **Grammarly** - Enhances grammar, tone, and clarity in writing for professional or creative purposes. https://www.grammarly.com

7. **Surfer SEO** - Combines content writing with keyword optimization for improved search engine rankings. https://surferseo.com

8. **Pictory** - Converts long text or video content into short, engaging video clips. https://pictory.ai

9. **Lumen5** - Automates the creation of videos from text, blog posts, or scripts. https://www.lumen5.com

10. **Synthesia** - Creates AI-generated videos with realistic avatars and voiceovers. https://www.synthesia.io

11. **Descript** - Edits videos and podcasts, transcribes audio, and generates subtitles. https://www.descript.com

12. **Murf.ai** - Produces high-quality AI-generated voiceovers for videos or presentations. https://murf.ai

13. **Quillbot** - Paraphrases, summarizes, and improves writing style. https://quillbot.com

14. **ContentBot** - Generates blog posts, product descriptions, and social media captions. https://contentbot.ai

15. **MarketMuse** - Optimizes content strategies by analyzing competitors and content gaps. https://www.marketmuse.com

16. **Adobe Firefly** - Enhances image and video creation with generative AI features. https://www.adobe.com/sensei/generative-ai/firefly.html

17. **DeepL Write** - Improves text translation and writing fluency in multiple languages. https://www.deepl.com/write

18. **INK** - Combines SEO, writing, and AI optimization for digital content creation. https://inkforall.com

19. **Runway ML** - Creates visuals, animations, and edits video content with AI assistance. https://runwayml.com

20. **Midjourney AI** - Generates high-quality digital art and visual content based on text prompts. https://www.midjourney.com

21. **Suno AI** - Creates voiceovers, music, and speech-based AI content. https://www.suno.ai

22. **Gamma AI** - Generates visually engaging presentations and slide decks using simple inputs. https://gamma.app

23. **Snazzy AI** - Crafts marketing content like email campaigns, landing pages, and ads. https://www.snazzy.ai

24. **Bard Gemini AI** - Google's conversational AI for generating content, summarizing information, and answering complex questions with enhanced web integration. https://bard.google.com

Most of these AI tools are free to use. Although they have paid features, mastering prompt engineering can help you to maximize their benefits, create income or optimize your career or business without having to pay to start with.

With one AI tool or a few others, (just as I used only ChatGPT *freely* to create and refine this book), you can achieve your goal (s).

And then you may get the paid features to solidify your work. With machine prompt engineering, you can also understand and deploy your creator mentality and consciousness

By the time you are reading this, these AI must have improved and other AI tools may have been created but the basic uses for content creation are the same.

> *"Machine Prompt Engineering is not just a skill—it's a gateway to leveraging AI for endless possibilities."*

Chapter Four: The Creator Consciousness – Transform Challenges into Opportunities

In life, the way you perceive situations determines your reality. Adopting the **Creator Mentality and Consciousness** is about shifting from a fixed mindset or victim mentality into a state of empowerment and possibility.

It's the conscious choice to see challenges as opportunities for growth and transformation rather than as obstacles that define or limit you.

The Creator Mentality empowers you to take control of your life, embrace your mistakes, and harness your innate ability to change your reality. It's the mindset that allows you to stop blaming others and start creating solutions or focusing on your opportunities or solutions.

Understanding the Creator Mentality

The Creator Mentality is rooted in the belief that **you are the architect of your life and largely responsible for whatever happens to you through your choices and understanding (actions and inactions).**

It challenges the notion that life happens *to* you and replaces it with the belief that life **happens *for* you,**

giving you the tools and lessons you need to create a better future right from the present.

When you operate from this mindset, you:

1. **Own your mistakes**: Acknowledge and apologize to yourself and others for past missteps or mistakes.

2. **Embrace your power**: Recognize that you have the ability to change any aspect of your reality.

3. **See possibilities**: View challenges as opportunities to innovate and grow or evolve.

4. **Ask the right questions**: Instead of feeling stuck, you often ask, *"How can I out create this problem?""what can I do to change my situation" "who can I partner with"* etc

The creator mentality and consciousness is a powerful tool in today's world of constant disruption and challenges.

Moving Beyond the Victim Mentality

A victim mentality keeps you trapped in a cycle of blame and helplessness. You may find yourself saying:

- "This always happens to me."
- "I can't change my circumstances."

- "If only things were different, I'd succeed."

These thoughts limit your potential and shift your focus away from solutions. The Creator Mentality, on the other hand, reframes these thoughts into empowering ones such as:

- *"This challenge is teaching me something valuable."*
- *"What can I do right now to change my situation?"*
- *"How can I turn this setback into a stepping stone?"*
- *What do I focus on to change my situation?*
- *What can I create while I am still here or in this satiation?*
- *What approaches do I need to change or adopt?*

Answering any of these transformative questions correctly will help you to navigate through your challenges to create the life you truly desire.

The Power of Vision in Creator Consciousness

Creators don't just react to life; they envision a better future and take proactive steps to make it a reality. This vision becomes their guiding light, helping them to stay focused and motivated even in the face of adversity.

Practical Steps to Develop Vision:

1. **Identify your desired outcome:** What do you truly want in your relationships, career, wellness, or impact?

2. **Visualize success:** Spend time imagining yourself achieving your goals.

3. **Break it down:** Create actionable steps to bring your vision to life.

4. **Stay adaptable:** Be willing to adjust your path as you learn and grow.

Your vision is the future you are creating and you must constantly nurture it on a daily basis. Your vision will attack challenges but should not destroy it.

Action Steps: *Develop a vision of the life you want to live. Write it or create the image and constantly put it in front of you.*

Leveraging Challenges to Create Success

Every challenge carries within it the seed of opportunity. The Creator Mentality teaches you to look for these seeds and use them to grow.

Example Scenarios:

- **In relationships:** A painful breakup can teach you about your values and help you attract a partner aligned with them.

- **In wellness:** Health setbacks can inspire you to adopt a healthier lifestyle or explore new wellness practices.

- **In your career:** Job loss can push you to pursue a passion or start a business you've always dreamed of or learn a new skill.

Action Step: When faced with a problem, ask yourself: *"What can I learn from this? How can I use it to create something better?"*

How to Cultivate the Creator Mentality

Here are five practical ways to cultivate the creator mentality and consciousness.

1. **Shift your perspective:** Practice seeing problems as opportunities.
    - Replace *"Why is this happening to me?"* with *"What can I do with this?"*

2. **Practice self-compassion:** Forgive yourself for mistakes and focus on the lessons learned.

3. **Develop resilience:** Learn to bounce back from setbacks quickly by focusing on your goals.

4. **Adopt a proactive mindset:** Take responsibility for your actions and decisions, knowing they shape your future.

5. **Stay curious:** Constantly ask, *"How can I outcreate this situation?"*

Action Steps: Speak the following statement loudly: say it this way:

"I am responsible for whatever happens to me."

"I have the power to change my circumstances and reality on a daily basis."

"I am identifying and creating the opportunities to achieve my goals."

Do it right now.

Converting Challenges into Opportunities: The Creator's Perspective

Challenges are not obstacles; they are stepping stones that guide you toward your destination. Tribulations, no matter how difficult, often carry the seeds of transformation, pushing you to grow, learn, and innovate.

This mindset—where challenges are seen as opportunities—lies at the heart of the Creator Mentality.

Hope is more than a feeling; it's a plan. A plan that drives action and fuels resilience. That's why I believe in building and working with systems. Systems provide structure, consistency, and clarity, even in the face of adversity. Challenges are like ingredients, essential for "cooking" your success. Instead of focusing on the discomfort they bring, look at what they can teach you and how they can propel you forward.

To convert challenges into opportunities, start by shifting your focus. Look beyond the difficulty or offense you might feel and resist the urge for revenge or blame. Instead, channel your energy into what you can learn and what you can do in the present moment to advance. Each day, take small, purposeful actions that align with your long-term vision.

Equally important is valuing the small things. Success is rarely built in one grand leap; it's the result of consistent, incremental progress. The small victories, the seemingly insignificant steps, are what ultimately create the big milestones in life. Celebrate them, learn from them, and let them build your confidence to tackle larger challenges.

When you adopt this mindset, challenges lose their power to paralyze you. Instead, they become catalysts for growth, helping you craft solutions, build resilience, and achieve your goals. Remember, the path to greatness is paved with trials, but each one is an opportunity to create something extraordinary.

By embracing this approach, you can transform adversity into the fuel that powers your journey toward success, fulfillment, and a better life. That's the essence of the Creator Mentality—turning every challenge into an opportunity for growth.

It is all about how you see the challenge or challenges and keep creating solutions, first inwardly and secondly, outwardly.

Evolving Through Social Media: A Gateway to Opportunity

Social media has transformed from a simple platform for connecting with family and friends into a multi-billion-dollar ecosystem.

Today, it serves as a powerful tool where individuals and businesses share ideas, build brands, and create economic opportunities. More than just a space for social interaction, social media has become a critical sub-sector of the digital economy, shaping the way we network, market, and conduct business on a global scale.

To harness the full potential of social media, it's essential to see it as more than just a place to scroll or post casually. Whether you're an entrepreneur, a content creator, or someone with an idea to share, your social media accounts can serve as a launchpad to amplify your voice and reach a worldwide audience. If you don't already have an account tailored to your professional goals, now is the time to create one. Use these platforms to build your network, promote your business, and bring your ideas to life.

Recognizing this, I've developed strategies to effectively leverage social media for advancing my projects, marketing my books, and sharing my ideas with a global audience.

By aligning with the Creator Mentality, you too can maximize the benefits of social media. Whether it's growing your business, establishing your personal brand, or connecting with like-minded individuals, social media offers endless opportunities for those willing to embrace its potential.

There are many people who have started their businesses online through social media before they finally evolve to establish a physical office or store. This is because social media has evolved into a creative space for everyone to thrive.

Start viewing your social media presence not as a pastime but as a strategic asset. With intentional effort, consistency, and creativity, social media can become a transformative tool to help you achieve your goals and thrive in the digital economy.

Creators are the Most Successful People

Those who embrace the Creator Mentality and Consciousness are often the most successful because they:

- See beyond immediate obstacles.
- Innovate in the face of adversity.
- Inspire others with their resilience and vision.
- Continuously evolve and improve.

Those with the Creator Mentality do not just solve problems; they create new possibilities and opportunities that transform their lives and the lives of others.

Final Thought

The Creator Mentality is not just a mindset; it's a way of life. It's the conscious decision to rise above limitations and become the driver of your destiny. Life may throw challenges your way, but with the Creator Consciousness, you hold the power to turn them into opportunities for extraordinary growth, impact, and success. See yourself as the creator of your reality, and watch how your life transforms in unimaginable ways. Make the shift today. Confess it with your words right now: "I am a creator of my life and circumstances"

> *"Those with the Creator Mentality do not just solve problems; they create new possibilities and opportunities that transform their lives and the lives of others."*

Chapter Five: The Good Life Philosophy – Crafting and Sharing Your Path to Success

Life becomes meaningful when it's guided by a philosophy that aligns with your values, dreams, and experiences.

Just like everything else, the **Good Life Philosophy** is an art of crafting your personal framework for defining and achieving success, happiness, and fulfillment. It's not only a tool for self-improvement but also a resource you can share to inspire and empower others.

This chapter explores how to create your Good Life Philosophy, leverage it to transform your life, and monetize it as a tool for teaching and guiding others.

What is the Good Life Philosophy?

The Good Life Philosophy is a set of principles and beliefs that guide your decisions, actions, and goals. It's a reflection of what has worked for you and what you believe can create a fulfilling life.

At its core, it's about:

1. Identifying what matters most to you.

2. Documenting your values, strategies, and lessons learned.
3. Using this framework to create a life aligned with your vision of success.

To create your own or adopt a good life philosophy, you need to understand why you have to do so.

Why Create a Good Life Philosophy?

- **Clarity:** It provides a clear roadmap for achieving your goals and staying true to your values.

- **Focus:** It eliminates distractions and keeps you aligned with your purpose.

- **Impact:** It allows you to inspire others by sharing a proven system for success.

- **Income:** It can be monetized as a teaching tool, workshop, book, or online course.

By knowing the 'why' behind your good life philosophy, you can then master the steps to creating and working it flexibly.

Steps to Create Your Good Life Philosophy

1. **Reflect on Your Journey:**
    - Identify key experiences that shaped your values and beliefs.
    - Highlight successes and failures, and extract the lessons they taught you.

2. **Define Your Core Values:**
    - What principles guide your decisions?
    - Examples: Integrity, growth, empathy, perseverance.

3. **Envision Your Ideal Life:**
    - What does success look like for you?
    - Consider areas like health, relationships, career, and personal growth.

4. **Develop Actionable Strategies:**
    - Break down your philosophy into steps or habits that can be implemented daily.

5. **Document Your Philosophy:**
    - Write it in a clear, inspiring, and practical format.

- Consider creating a manifesto, book, or digital resource.

With the above, you can begin to monetize your good life philosophy and help other people to grow and establish their successes.

Monetizing Your Good Life Philosophy

Sharing your philosophy can open doors to both personal fulfillment and financial opportunities. Here's how:

1. **Write a Book or E-Book:**
   - Publish your philosophy as a guide or memoir.
   - Use platforms like Amazon Kindle or Gumroad etc.

2. **Create Online Courses:**
   - Develop workshops or training programs based on your philosophy.
   - Use platforms like Udemy or Teachable.

3. **Host Webinars or Seminars:**
   - Teach your philosophy to live audiences, both online and offline.

4. **Launch a Coaching Program:**

- Offer one-on-one or group coaching sessions to help others implement your philosophy or that good philosophy to change their lives.

5. **Develop Content for Social Media:**

    - Share bite-sized lessons from your philosophy on Instagram, LinkedIn, or TikTok.

Apart from showing my good life philosophy briefly in the next chapter, there is a need to show you a broader view or example of a good life philosophy.

Examples of a Good Life Philosophy in Action

Here are a few example of a good life philosophy by different people:

- **The Power of Persistence:** A philosophy focused on resilience and consistency. Its creator offers coaching and courses on how to overcome setbacks and achieve goals.

- **Minimalism for Fulfillment:** A philosophy advocating for simplicity to create a life of purpose. Its creator runs a successful blog and workshops.

- **Mindfulness for Success:** A philosophy combining meditation and productivity strategies.

Its creator monetizes through retreats, books, and online content.

- **Transformative Leadership:** A philosophy that proves that the core essence of mankind is leadership leading to empathy, unity, love and a peaceful world. And with a universal time innovation strategy to establish leadership excellence. The creator monetizes through retreats, seminars, books, and online content.

Having seen these examples, you need some tips to craft and to start practicing or showcasing your good life philosophy.

Pro Tips for Teaching Your Philosophy

Personally, I am using these tips:

1. **Start Small:** Begin by sharing your philosophy with close friends, on social media, or as blog posts.

2. **Gather Feedback:** Refine your philosophy based on the reactions and results of others.

3. **Use AI Tools:** Leverage AI like ChatGPT to generate engaging content, design courses, or refine your writing.

4. **Build a Community:** Create a network of people who resonate with your philosophy and want to learn more.

The world is waiting to hear from you and to make it a better place for peaceful prosperity through your conscious enablement and philosophy.

The Ripple Effect of Sharing Your Philosophy

When you teach your Good Life Philosophy, you're not just sharing a set of principles; you're creating a legacy.

By helping others achieve the success they desire, you amplify your impact and contribute to a cycle of growth and empowerment.

As you grow, so does your philosophy. It evolves with your experiences, making it an ever-expanding tool for transformation—for you and those you inspire.

Final Thought

Creating and sharing your Good Life Philosophy is not just about achieving your own dreams—it's about lighting the path for others. By documenting what works, teaching it, and monetizing it, you're building a life of purpose and impact while empowering others to do the same.

Start today. Reflect on your journey, define your values, and craft a philosophy that transforms lives—yours and the world.

My Good Life Philosophy

Following from the above as a perfect example, here is a brief analysis of my good life philosophy and discovery.

1. **By Journey:**
    - Over many years, I suffered hardship and struggles like anyone in an environment of systemic failure and high level of leadership mediocrity. But this, instead of breaking me, helped me to search for and discover why people behave the way they do. This has shaped my values and beliefs.
    - I discovered the universal principle of time innovation which I call H-TIPS (Human and Time Innovation Power System), which has the potential to transform mankind helping us to make the world a better and peaceful place in unity of mind and purpose. I learned that just using the principle will not bring you money but makes you safe, be of high moral standard, understanding and discernment and to establish your core essence in life which is leadership (for

empathy, love, creative success and transformation) in every area of life endeavour for self-actualization and impact. This is what we all need and desire in life.

2. **My Core Values:**

    o The principles of my decisions are empathy, integrity, unity or partnership and knowledge; thus helping me and others to grow and reach our innate potential through self-reliance and interdependence.

3. **My Ideal Life: what success looks like to me.**

    o Success is rooted in the understanding and knowledge to be safe, healthy and productive, building healthy relationships (supporting one another without reservation) for personal growth or collective success. This makes success a going concern instead of something static or fixed.

4. **Develop Actionable Strategies:**

    o To be safe and to transform your life; I have adopted the principle of H-TIPS and started using it daily to establish my leadership prowess for success.

    o Life is lived daily and so is success- helps there is need for principles to help us establish our safety, health, venture, productivity and relationship on a daily basis or as a daily routine.

5. **Documenting My Philosophy:**

    o   I have written my good life philosophy in a clear, inspiring, and practical format (that's why you are reading it right now).

    o   I have created a manifesto (policy programs etc), and books with many digital resources to showcase my good life philosophy and principle of H-TIPS.

In 2012, I started looking earnestly for the reason why many good people fall prey to evil or lose self control and why there is so much ignorance, greed and pride are highly expressive in the life of many people and the lot of mankind.

Then in 2016, I discovered the missing link (a universal principle of nature) which I now call H-TIPS (Human and Time Innovation Power System).

Using H-TIPS will unite mankind and help us to establish transformative leadership and sustainable change to make the world a better place.

H-TIPS do not only help us to establish our safety and leadership authority over our lives and the earth; it is a channel to personal development and a new world of peaceful prosperity. Start using H-TIPS today. It is FREE!

In the following chapter, I will expand with the same details the principle of the universal principle of time- H-TIPS and how it came about.

> *"The Good Life Philosophy is a set of principles and beliefs that guide your decisions, actions, and goals. It's a reflection of what has worked for you and what you believe can create a fulfilling life"*

Chapter Six: My Journey – The Birth of a Transformative Idea

This is an opportunity for us to connect through shared experiences and principles. Life was not easy for me for many years chiefly because I grew up in an environment where people often felt powerless against life and their circumstances.

It was a society where having a college degree was seen as the ultimate key to success, where career achievements were mistaken for holistic fulfillment, and where having money often gave people a false sense of superiority.

In this setting, individual difference was discouraged, innovation was often viewed with suspicion, and those who dared to think differently were ostracized or detested.

It was also a society where people pursued their desires—even at the expense of their loved ones—with little or no accountability. You may often hear rhetoric like:

"I lived for myself alone- I don't care and I am not accountable to anyone",

"Iit doesn't matter how to make it to the top."

"Money is the ultimate goal; it matters if someone is hurt..." etc.

Most of these statements and the context in which they were used clearly denote mental depravity and mediocrity of human-person or group (involved) with obsolete or harmful religious or socio-economic and political beliefs. This mental backdrop, I discovered is the cause of of systemic challenges and it sparked a fire in me to find answers to some of the lingering generational questions such as:

- *Why do so many people struggle?*
- *Why do humans suffer in the midst of abundance?*
- *Why do people live with so much ignorance, greed and pride even with their high level of education?*
- *Why do good people suffer evil and are easily vulnerable to evil or death.*
- *And what can I do to help...?*
- *etc*

The Search for a Solution

The quest for answers consumed me for years- even my university degrees did not provide me the answers. I observed, reflected, and experimented, determined to uncover what was missing in the way people lived their lives.

Eventually, I discovered a universal principle of nature—something transformative and unifying—that I call **H-TIPS (Human and Time Innovation Power System).**

H-TIPS is more than a concept; it is a way to align human potential with the natural principles of life and the universe. It holds the power to unite humanity and create lasting change.

But this discovery was not without challenges. Many rejected it out rightly. After all, introducing a revolutionary idea—a paradigm shift from the status quo—is never easy. People tend to cling to the beliefs and mindsets they grew up with, whether rooted in tradition, religion, or societal norms. Change can feel threatening, even when it offers a better way forward.

I found solace in the understanding that what is unknown is often misunderstood or misused. So, I persevered, using and refining H-TIPS in my own life and sharing its transformative spark with others- including family and friends.

H-TIPS exposes the best time or hours (12noon and 12midnight) to use our creative energy (spoken words) in positive affirmation consciously for ourselves, family, leaders, city and nation on a daily basis. As simple as it seems, H-TIPS is very transformative and powerful. It has the potential to unite and transform mankind and our way of life or how we treat each other.

The challenge is that though supported by nature and scientific laws; most people may neglect using H-TIPS in search of jobs and money hoping to be safe and transformed just because they have good intentions, education, and great passion or technological gadgets.

Personal Development and Safety

H-TIPS does not only help us to take hold of our lives every day. It is about working more on yourself than on your job to attract success, remain safe, and refine your minds, expanding your leadership capacity.

Using H-TIPS helps us to transform our minds and exempt ourselves from evil on a daily basis. Against using H-TIPS, unfortunately, I have seen many good people die (some of them caught up by the mistakes or the evil plans of other people, just because they have not constantly deployed H-TIPS in their lives.

You don't want to think about this- there are unfortunate stories of many people who are suffering evil just because they have failed to use this universal principle of time innovation to take proper charge of their lives.

And since the universe responds mainly to laid down principles, just having great wishes, good intentions or great passion and even having lots of money or technology is not the fundamental solution but H-TIPS.

Leadership Prowess and Excellence

Using H-TIPS brings out our leadership prowess and capability including creative thinking and empathy. That's what the world needs right now.

With H-TIPS, it has been established that the core essence of mankind is leadership. This is to take leadership dominion of the earth and our lives with our creative energy via the instrumentality of time (the universal leadership hours) on a daily basis. It is a universal principle that has remained unchanged as long as time remains the same. And failure to do so is fundamental leadership failure.

In a social media post, I put up a question of "what the world needs most in one word". A lot of people gave their opinions such as "peace", "love", "humanity", "empathy", "tolerance", "God", "unity" "justice" etc.

I believe they were all right however, all they mentioned falls under "leadership". By establishing our core leadership responsibility we will have "peace", "love", "humanity", "empathy", "tolerance", "God", "unity" "justice" etc. And we make the world a better place. That is what H-TIPS embodies. All those who consistently use H-TIPS will not only be safe but establish leadership excellence in every area of life.

Re-Engineering the Universe with Your Creative Energy Prompts Daily

The following are creative prompts or affirmation you should make into the universe at the universal leadership hours:

- *I am not a victim but a creator of my circumstances, my day and my entire life.*

- *I am leading the world to greatness and making it a better place for this and future generations.*

- *Today, I exempt myself from all evil that may occur.*

- *Today I exempt these persons (names them) from all evil.*

- *I ask that the universe deliver the understanding that I and my loved ones need to stay healthy and productive or prosperous today.*

- *I speak into the lives of the leaders of this country, city or state (list their names) for health and understanding to do the right thing.*

Anyone striving for greatness and genuine success—while working to make the world a better place—must continually overcome the challenges of ignorance, greed, and pride (the IGP Crisis). H-TIPS provides a practical framework to consistently navigate and triumph over these obstacles. It has transformed my life, and it can do the same for you.

This is not just a philosophical theory; it's a proven approach. Don't simply take my word for it—test it yourself. Commit to applying H-TIPS consistently for at least 40 days to nine months.

You'll begin to notice a remarkable change in your thoughts, understanding, and ability to make decisions that stand for what is right. This transformation will empower you to influence positive change and build a better version of yourself. That's where the journey begins.

This is about constant change and realignment with your higher 'leadership' purpose from within. If you change, you will change the way you look at things and the things you look at will change. H-TIPS is the key to personal change and development from within for the best.

Consequently, the solution for human transformation and a peaceful world will be the same, free and easily applicable for and by everyone. It is H-TIPS. To know more about H-TIPS you can get any of my "books:

1. **"H-TIPS: a Bold Invention for Humanity"**
2. **"The Way Out for Mankind"**
3. **"Transformative Leadership Model"**
   Etc

Facing the Challenges

Some assumed that discovering H-TIPS would instantly make me wealthy or famous. But life does not work that way. Great ideas require time, effort, and resilience to take root. I knew that the first step toward change was starting with myself. If I wanted to create a lasting impact, I needed to refine my thoughts, align my actions with universal principles, and embody the change I wanted to see.

This journey was far from smooth. Support was scarce, and systemic failures seemed to close doors at every turn. Yet, I learned to adapt, to keep searching for new ways to scale my ideas.

When one plan failed, I didn't see it as a personal failure—it was just a strategy that didn't work. So, I tried again, each time learning and improving.

Embracing the Internet and AI

One of the turning points in my journey was embracing the power of the internet. I began publishing H-TIPS through books, articles, and online platforms. It was a new frontier for me, and I committed to learning the skills necessary to succeed in this digital world.

Another transformative tool in my journey has been AI, particularly ChatGPT. It played a pivotal role in helping me develop this book from start to finish. Using some principles of Machine Prompt engineering (which I showed earlier in this book), AI allowed me to articulate my thoughts clearly, structure my ideas effectively, and reach a wider audience.

The Lessons I Learned

Today, I'm proud that I never gave up. Despite the challenges, I clung to my vision, refining it and finding ways to share it with others. If you're reading this, know that this could be your story too.

In a world where systemic failures are common and support is limited, here is my advice to you:

1. **Keep Looking:** Explore every opportunity that comes your way. If one door closes, find another and open.

2. **Learn Continuously:** Stay curious and seek out new ways to grow and innovate.

3. **Leverage What You Have:** Use your unique skills, resources, and experiences to scale your ideas.

4. **Embrace Failure:** If a plan doesn't work, don't bicker or give up. Learn the lesson, adapt and move forward with a new plan. If a plan fails, it's not you who failed—it's just the strategy that needs adjusting.

In the above, you will find discipline, flexibility, perseverance, leadership, determination and motivation- the key ingredients that lead to success or personal development.

A Final Word

Discovering H-TIPS taught me that life is not about blaming others or feeling powerless. It's about seeing every challenge as an opportunity to create something better. And through persistence, self-reflection, and leveraging tools like AI, I've turned my vision into reality. This book is a product of that journey. It's a testament to what's possible when you refuse to give up, when you embrace innovation, and when you learn to leverage the resources available to you.

Let this be a reminder that you have the power to transform your life, create your own success, and help others along the way. The world is waiting for your unique contribution—don't hold back.

> *"With H-TIPS, it has been established that the core essence of mankind is leadership. This is to take leadership dominion of the earth and our lives with our creative energy via the instrumentality of time (the universal leadership hours) on a daily basis."*

Chapter Seven: Mastering Machine Prompt Engineering: Key to Innovation, Iteration, and Evolving

Mastering Machine Prompt Engineering, especially through AI tools, is not just about understanding how to use the technology—it's about tapping into a process of continuous self-improvement and adaptability.

Machine Prompt Engineering is a skill set designed to help you innovate, iterate, and evolve in every area of your life, creating and maximizing opportunities while advancing your personal life, business, and career.

Let's explore these three key interrelated concepts:

Innovation

Innovation is the spark that sets the journey in motion. It's about doing things differently, thinking outside the box, and creating new solutions to old problems. When you approach Machine Prompt Engineering with an innovative mindset, you unlock the ability to:

- Generate unique ideas and strategies for personal growth or business transformation.
- Discover new ways to use AI tools creatively, such as crafting prompts to design products,

solve complex problems, or simplify your workflow.
- Enhance your life by applying technology to everyday challenges, improving efficiency, and freeing up time for what truly matters.

The key to innovation is to remain curious and open-minded. Ask yourself, "What can I do differently today?" With this mindset, you'll always be ready to explore new horizons.

Iteration

Iteration is the process of refining and improving through practice and persistence. The true power of Machine Prompt Engineering lies in your ability to test, learn, and adjust. It's not about perfection from the start but about gradual improvement over time.

Here's how iteration works in practice:

- **Test your prompts:** Experiment with different approaches and refine them based on the output you receive from AI tools.

- **Learn from feedback:** Pay attention to what works and what doesn't, and use those insights to improve your future prompts.
- **Embrace failure as growth:** Mistakes or suboptimal results are not setbacks but opportunities to learn and grow.

Iteration is a cycle of continuous improvement. It ensures that every step you take brings you closer to mastering your craft and achieving your goals.

Evolving

Evolving is about growth—becoming a better version of yourself by embracing change and adapting to new circumstances. It's the culmination of innovation and iteration. With Machine Prompt Engineering, evolution happens in several dimensions:

- **Personal Growth:** Use prompts to gain clarity on your goals, plan your day, or overcome personal challenges. Over time, you'll notice a transformation in your mindset and habits.
- **Professional Development:** Leverage AI to develop new skills, expand your expertise, or refine your business strategies. As you evolve, so does your ability to compete and succeed in a rapidly changing world.
- **Consciousness Expansion:** Evolving is not just about external achievements; it's also about internal growth. By embracing a creator mentality, you shift from being reactive to proactive, taking charge of your destiny.

Evolution is an ongoing process. It's about committing to lifelong learning and continuous self-improvement, knowing that every step forward, no matter how small, contributes to your journey.

The Power of Integration

When you combine innovation, iteration, and evolving, you unlock the full potential of Machine Prompt Engineering and the creator mentality. These principles are interconnected:

- **Innovation** inspires action.
- **Iteration** refines that action into success.
- **Evolving** ensures that success is sustainable and transformative.

By mastering these concepts, you don't just use AI—you become a creator in every sense of the word, capable of shaping your reality and advancing your life, business, and career with purpose and precision.

> *"Machine Prompt Engineering is a skill set designed to help you innovate, iterate, and evolve in every area of your life, creating and maximizing opportunities while advancing your personal life, business, and career. "*

Chapter Eight: Conclusion – Embrace the Power Within

Everything in this book represents the power of AI (through machine prompt engineering), the creator consciousness and crafting a good life philosophy for success and impact.

Through the pages of this book, I have not only shown how to maximize the power of AI as a machine prompt engineer but how to turn around your life because you have the power to do so.

We have explored the boundless opportunities that exist in the modern world—opportunities that are no longer reserved for the privileged few but are accessible to anyone willing to learn, adapt, and act.

From mastering the art of Machine Prompt Engineering to adopting a mindset rooted in the **Creator Mentality**, this book has provided you with the tools, strategies, and philosophies to not only navigate the digital age but thrive in it.

The Power of AI in Your Hands

Artificial Intelligence is no longer just a futuristic concept; it is a present-day enabler of success. By learning how to communicate with AI through precise prompts, you hold the key to unlocking limitless possibilities in content creation, business development, and personal growth.

Machine Prompt Engineering is not just a skill; it's a superpower. It empowers you to:

- Automate and optimize repetitive tasks.
- Enhance creativity and productivity.
- Scale your ventures faster than ever imagined.

This is not the future—it is now. And it is yours to command.

The Power of Your Mind

Beyond the tools and technologies, the foundation of lasting success lies within **you**. Throughout this journey, I have emphasized the importance of mindset. The shift from a fixed or victim mentality to a **Creator Mentality** is the cornerstone of transformation.

You have the power to change your reality, no matter the challenges you face. By leveraging obstacles as opportunities and embracing a vision of new possibilities, you can create the life you desire. Remember:

- **You are not powerless.** You are the architect of your destiny.

- **Your circumstances don't define you.** Your actions do.

- **Your failures are not final.** They are lessons guiding you to a better path.

The Good Life Philosophy

Life's challenges often lead us to discover universal truths and principles that shape who we are. Your experiences, both good and bad, can become the foundation of a personal philosophy that guides you toward success.

By reflecting on what has worked for you and sharing it with others, you not only create value for yourself but also inspire others to transform their lives.

Your Journey Ahead

The journey doesn't end here—it begins here. Armed with the knowledge and strategies shared in this book, you have everything you need to:

- Embrace and master AI tools to unlock online wealth.
- Shift your mindset to align with growth, resilience, and creativity.
- Use your experiences to craft a life philosophy that serves you and others.
- Turn your ideas into income, your challenges into triumphs, and your dreams into reality.

The path ahead may not always be easy, but it is always worth it. Success is not about the destination—it's about who you become along the way.

Final Words

Through the challenges I faced, I discovered the universal principles of **H-TIPS (Human and Time Innovation Power System)** and the transformative power of aligning with nature's laws. You, too, can create lasting change in your life and in the lives of others by embracing these principles and using them as a guiding light.

As you close this book, remember: you hold the power to rewrite your story. Every obstacle is an opportunity, every failure a stepping stone, and every idea a seed for greatness. Take what you have learned, apply it with intention, and share it boldly with the world.

The future belongs to those who act. The time is now.

Your Success Friend,

Ijigban Daniel Oketa

About the Author

Ijigban Daniel Oketa is an innovator, entrepreneur, and thought leader passionate about ethical AI, digital, human and systemic transformation.

As the inventor of *H-TIPS (Human and Time Innovation Power System)*, he is dedicated to promoting morality, safety, and leadership excellence.

With over two decades of experience in entrepreneurship, business consulting, and education, Oketa has empowered individuals and organizations to align with nature's principles for impactful change and sustainable growth.

He is also an advocate for digital innovation, leveraging AI and technology to optimize personal experiences and professional outcomes. Through his writing, speaking, and mentorship, Ijigban inspires others to embrace their potential and create meaningful success in every aspect of life for self actualization and to make the world a better place.

About the Book

Master the Art of Machine Prompt Engineering: Unlock AI for Life, Business, and Career Success is your ultimate guide to thriving in the digital age. Whether you're looking to boost your career, grow your business, or transform your personal life, this book equips you with the tools to unlock the power of Artificial Intelligence (AI) and achieve unparalleled success. This transformative guide will teach you how to:

- Harness the power of **Machine Prompt Engineering** (no coding required) to leverage AI in any language, including English, Arabic, Spanish, French, and Mandarin.
- Cultivate a **creator mentality and consciousness** to establish your unique value and stand out in the digital landscape.
- Define and live by your **personal philosophy for success**, paving the way for growth and fulfillment.
- Turn challenges into opportunities, and ideas into income—both online and offline.

Discover the key to merging the power of AI with the limitless potential of your mind. AI is only as effective as the prompts you craft, and this book shows you how to master the art of storytelling, strategic thinking, and creativity to unlock its full potential.

Packed with actionable insights on Machine Prompt Engineering, content creation, and mindset transformation, this guide will empower you to:

- Enhance your **personal life**, **career**, and **business**.
- Build a future where your ideas and efforts lead to sustainable success.

Whether you're an entrepreneur, a professional, a student, or someone with big dreams, **Master the Art of Machine Prompt Engineering** offers practical tools and proven strategies to help you reshape your life and achieve lasting impact.

Join My Global Online Community & Newsletter

Connect with like-minded individuals, build impactful partnerships, and stay ahead with the latest AI trends, wealth-building strategies, and profit-making ideas.

Be part of the movement—sign up today!

@
www.haatglobal.com

or you may follow me on Social Media
@ Ijigban Daniel Oketa
@Idoketa
@HisLordship_idOketa

Partnership Opportunities

If you're interested in collaborating to promote the paperback or exploring other business opportunities, I'd love to hear from you.

No matter where you are, let's connect and create meaningful partnerships.

Feel free to reach me on mobile or WhatsApp at **+234 703 738 4814**.

Let's make great things happen together!

NOTES

www.ingramcontent.com/pod-product-compliance
Lightning Source LLC
Chambersburg PA
CBHW070357230526
45471CB00006B/2610